Master Menu Cookbook

The Organized Way to Cook

৪০০৪

Marie Calder Ricks

First edition.

Cover design by Marie C. Ricks and Thomas E. Ricks.
Copyright page artwork by Thomas E. Ricks,
www.tomricks.com.
Interior artwork by Marie C. Ricks.

Comments or suggestions are greatly appreciated:
www.houseoforder.com.

Also visit ***www.houseoforder.com*** for more
information concerning your organizational needs,
to purchase organizational products, schedule
a personal consultation, speaking engagement,
or educational seminar.

ISBN-10 0-9788579-2-5
ISBN-13 978-0-9788579-2-9

Also by Marie Calder Ricks:

House of Order Handbook
200+ pages of easy-to-follow instructions for setting up and maintaining an orderly home. This trade paperback includes some 80+ worksheets to help organize your paperwork, finances, and shopping needs. It teaches principles that work!

House of Order Handbook CD 82+ worksheets from the _House of Order Handbook_ in .pdf file format for convenient reprinting on your home computer. It will make keeping organized a breeze as you work through each and every organization project.

Project Organization, Quick and Easy Ways to Organize Your Life
170+ pages of effective personal and home organization projects for home managers in all seasons of their lives. Available @ _www.shadowmountain.com_ or at your favorite bookstore.

Stay-At-Home Housecleaning Plan Packet 150+ index cards which detail the important daily, weekly, and more complex housework projects to keep your house neat and clean all the time. _Instructions included._

Working Person's Housecleaning Plan Packet 165+ index cards which detail the essential housework projects in a sequential manner to accommodate the more chaotic life and still keep the house neat and clean. _Instructions included._

Teaching Children to Work Packet 150+ index cards which detail the vital skills children and/or teenagers need to survive in the real world as independent adults. _Instructions included._

Family Information Binder Kit One 1" view binder and 75+ useful printed forms for a family of eight to keep track of the important information needed to run a family. _Instructions included._

Cleaning Standards Cards Five 8-1/2" x 11" heavy-duty laminated sheets, printed on both sides, which detail the essentials needed to get household jobs done right (whether you want the rooms "fast" cleaned, first side, or "deep" cleaned, second side).

See **_www.houseoforder.com_** to order these items.

Master Menu Cookbook

Table of Contents

Table of Contents

Master Menu Cookbook

Introduction

    The concept of the "Master Menu" is simple. Decide once and for all which main meals you will serve for a four-week period, twenty-eight main meals in all. Then use this "Master Menu" as a basis for planning a vegetable and fruit for the main meal each day of the week, one bread per day for your family if you have hearty eaters or teenagers, and one dessert to supplement meals as necessary. The "Master Menu" rotation is used over and over again, month after month. The same principle can be applied for breakfasts and lunches, although usually seven different meals, or one kind per day of the week, suits both these meals.

    The process is best done by having a family council and soliciting the family's interest. What are the favorite meals of each member of the family? It is surprising to learn family members feel some frustration that "the cook" keeps serving a meal which they detest and doesn't regularly serve their favorites. When they are involved in choosing the "Master Menu" meals, they feel more a part of the decisions and are more likely to support a less-favored meal when they find their own favorites have a special place on the menu. In addition, occasionally using your husband's favorite recipes makes that day of the week special for him. He deserves it and the rest of the family can learn from this variety, too.

    It is also helpful to give each day of the week a special name. This facilitates the initial planning and helps keep the specific menus in your head. For instance, Mondays are long days for most home managers. Calling this day the "Quick" day and preparing speedy meals with a minimum amount of ingredients and preparation time will help end the first work day of the week on an upbeat note. Tuesday might be "Mexican" day, Wednesday for "Poultry" meals, "Beef" for Thursdays, and Friday as "Italian" night. It is easy to see how quickly four meals in each of these categories might be chosen by the family. Saturday lunch might be a family favorite which none never tire of such as some variety of "hamburgers" with

Introduction

Saturday evening reserved for an "Easy" meal, maybe a cleanout of the refrigerator and prepared eggs of some type. Sunday brings "Soups" and sandwiches for lunch and "Breakfast for Dinner" in the evening.

Rotating through the 28 meals keeps the menus fresh and interesting and yet provides relief for the cook from the eternal question, "What are we having for dinner tonight?" Soon the family will know Tuesdays are for Mexican meals and will anticipate a South of the Border favorite along with buttered corn, cornbread, and mandarin oranges, for example.

Once the "Master Menu" is prepared, long-term shopping becomes much easier. When mandarin oranges come on sale, you can purchase fifty-two cans because you know you will be needing one can each week for Tuesday night's meals. When frozen corn is reduced in price, you can stock up your freezer, should you have one; or alternatively, get four flats of canned corn for your cupboards. Each and every time you buy for the whole year, that is one less item you shop for each week at the store. Soon your meals become easier and easier to prepare, and regular shopping is almost reduced to purchasing perishable foods.

It is helpful when preparing meats to think four meals at a time. The same "taco" meat recipe can be used once on soft tortillas, once on hard tacos, another time in enchiladas, and lastly as sloppy joes. When the meat is cooked, four quantities might be prepared and three put in the freezer. One preparation time and four meals are pretty much done. Then when the week begins, your frozen "taco" meat comes out for thawing and meal preparation.

Your "Italian" meat sauce might be prepared in the same way for Friday nights. Four quantities are prepared at the same time and three are frozen. The meat sauce is removed from the freezer on Monday and prepared along with a pasta on Fridays. One week it is noodles, one week macaroni, the third week lasagna and the fourth spaghetti.

The stress of meals is gone, a system is in place that works well, and everyone is pleased and feels more secure. Each day of the week brings its own vegetables, fruit, bread, and dessert. Everyone knows what's for dinner and general nutrition is improved.

Occasionally changes are made when a holiday ham needs using up or the mood calls for a spontaneous menu; but in general, the days of the week are structured in their meal orientation and preparation.

So enjoy this collection of "Master Menu" recipes that have worked well for me week after week, year after year. I have shared recipes for each day of the week, several good recipes for bulk cooking of meats, and other recipes which save me much time and trouble.

~Marie

Sample of Master Menu – Main Meals

Day/Name	Main Dish	Bread	Vegetable	Fruit
Monday	Pork & Bean Casserole	Honey Toast	Celery	Mandarin Oranges
Quick	Crescent Casserole			
	French Fry Burger Pie			
	Yakamish			
Tuesday	Soft Tacos	Cornbread	Corn	Peaches
Mexican	Chili & Chips			
	Enchiladas			
	Hard Tacos			
Wednesday	Oven Chicken Casserole	Biscuits	Carrots	Bananas
Poultry	Chicken Macaroni			
	Tuna Noodle			
	Luscious Lemon Chicken			
Thursday	Porcupine Meatballs	Rolls	Beans	Pears
Beef	Meatloaf/Rice			
	Primary Five-Hour Stew			
	No-Peek Casserole			
Friday	Spaghetti	Bread Sticks	Salad	Pineapple
Italian	Macaroni Beef			
	Lazy Day Lasagna			
	Mock Stroganoff			
Saturday	Sloppy Joes	Fried Potatoes	Peas	Apples
Easy	Hamburgers			
	Meatball Heroes			
	Chicken Gumbo Burgers			
Eggs	Fried Eggs	Toast	Celery	Orange Julius
	Cyclops	- -		
	Scrambled Eggs	Toast		
	Boiled Eggs	Toast		
Sunday	Bean w/ Bacon Soup	Toasted Cheese	Cucumbers	Peaches
Soup	Chicken Noodle Soup			
	Tomato Soup			
	Vegetable Beef Soup			
Breakfast	French Toast	- -	Carrots	Applesauce
for Dinner	Hootenany	- -		
	Pancakes	- -		
	Waffles	- -		

Sample of Master Menu – Breakfasts and Lunches

Day	Breakfast	Day	Lunch
Monday	Swedish Bread	**Monday**	Tuna Sandwiches
	Orange Juice		Carrots
	Milk		Milk
Tuesday	Cold Cereal	**Tuesday**	Peanut Butter & Jelly
	Grape Juice		Celery
	Milk		Milk
Wednesday	Swedish Bread	**Wednesday**	Egg Salad Sandwiches
	Orange Juice		Carrots
	Milk		Milk
Thursday	Cold Cereal	**Thursday**	Bologna Sandwiches
	Grape Juice		Cucumbers
	Milk		Milk
Friday	Swedish Bread	**Friday**	Roast Beef Sandwiches
	Orange Juice		Carrots
	Milk		Chocolate Milk
Saturday	Granola	**Saturday**	Sloppy Joes
	Raisins		Hamburgers
	Peanuts		Meatball Heroes
	Milk		Chicken Gumbo Burgers
Sunday	Coffee Cake	**Sunday**	Bean w/ Bacon Soup
	French Puffs		Chicken Noodle Soup
	Orange Julius Muffins		Tomato Soup
	Bannack		Vegetable Beef Soup

Master Menu Cookbook © Marie Calder Ricks/House of Order

PORK & BEAN CASSEROLE

1 lb. ground beef, cooked

4 t sugar

2 t *taco seasoning mix (pg. 44)*

1 t molasses (optional)

2 t white vinegar

1 t Worcestershire sauce

2 - 16 oz. cans pork & beans

1 – 10-3/4 oz. can tomato
  soup

2 c crushed potato chips

Mix ingredients in 9" x 13" casserole dish; top with potato chips. Bake at 350 degrees, 25-30 minutes. Serves 6.

CRESCENT CASSEROLE

1-1/2 lb. hamburger, cooked
1 t onion powder
2 T parsley flakes
4 - 8 oz. cans tomato sauce
2 c water
1/2 c grated cheese, any kind
4 c *Make-a-Mix (pg. 42)* mixed
    with 1 c milk

In 9" x 13" casserole dish, mix meat, sauce, spices, water. Top with cheese. Bake at 350 degrees 20 minutes. Top meat sauce with spooned-on biscuit mixture. Bake additional 20 minutes. Serves 6.

Monday

FRENCH FRY BURGER PIE

2 lb. ground beef, cooked
2 t powdered onion
2 10-3/4 oz. cans tomato
  soup
2/3 c catsup
1 20-oz. package frozen "thin"
  French-fried potatoes

Stir together meat, soup, catsup, spices, and frozen French fries. Put in 9" x 13" baking dish. Bake in 350-degree oven for 25-30 minutes. Serves 6.

YAKAMISH

1/4 c finely chopped onion
1 lb. ground beef, cooked
1 c raw carrot, shredded
4 c cooked rice

Mix ground beef, onion, carrot, and rice. Heat and serve with soy sauce. Serves 6.

SOFT TACOS

2 c *taco meat* *(pg. 43)*, heated
12 flour tortillas, warmed
   and buttered on one side

Spread meat on buttered
   tortillas.

Garnish with:
2 c shredded lettuce
2 c chopped tomatoes
2 c shredded cheese
2 c chopped onions

Serves 6.

Tuesday

CHILI & CHIPS

1-16 oz. can pork & beans
1-16 oz. can chili

1-10 oz. package Fritos

2 c shredded lettuce
2 c chopped tomatoes
2 c shredded cheese

Heat pork & beans and chili. Serve over Fritos on individual plates. Garnish with lettuce, tomatoes, and cheese. Serves 6.

ENCHILADAS

12 flour tortillas, buttered
2 c *taco meat (pg. 43)*, heated
2 T flour
2 T margarine
1/8 t paprika
1/4 t salt
1 c milk

Spread taco meat on tortillas. Roll up and put in 9" x 13" casserole dish. Combine white sauce ingredients in large glass cup. Stir thoroughly with beaters. Microwave 1 minute on HIGH. Stir. Repeat three times or until thickened. Pour white sauce over enchiladas in casserole dish. Cover and heat for 20-25 minutes in 350-degree oven. Serves 6.

HARD TACOS

2 c *taco meat* *(pg. 43)*, heated
12 hard taco shells

2 c shredded lettuce
2 c chopped tomatoes
2 c shredded cheese

Make tacos and enjoy.
Serves 6.

OVEN CHICKEN CASSEROLE

Wash 1-1/2 c rice and spread in
     large, greased dripper pan.

Mix: 1 10-3/4 oz. can cream
               of mushroom soup
          2 cans water
          2 chicken bouillon cubes

in glass cup and cook 2 minutes
on HIGH in microwave. Pour over
rice. Arrange meaty parts of
2 fryer chickens, salted, on top of
rice. Sprinkle with 2 T dry onion
soup mix. Bake, covered, for
1-1/2 hours in 325-degree oven.
Uncover last ten minutes to
brown. Serves 6.

CHICKEN MACARONI CASSEROLE

1-1/2 c dry macaroni, cooked and drained

1/2 t vinegar

1 10-3/4 oz. can cream of chicken soup

1/2 c milk

1 c cubed, cooked chicken

1/2 c mayonnaise

Mix above ingredients and place in casserole. Cover tightly with foil. Bake in 325-degree oven for 25-30 minutes. Serves 6.

Wednesday

TUNA NOODLE CASSEROLE

Cook 3-1/2 c noodles, drain

Combine cooked noodles &
  1 6-oz. can tuna
  1/2 c mayonnaise
  1 10-3/4 oz. can cream of
    mushroom soup
  1/2 c milk

Turn into a casserole dish.
Top with 1/2 c crushed potato
chips. Bake uncovered at 325
degrees for 25-30 minutes.
Serves 6.

LUSCIOUS LEMON CHICKEN

2 lbs. chicken parts

1 10-3/4 oz. can cream of
   chicken soup

2 T lemon juice

1/2 t paprika

1/8 t dry tarragon leaves,
   crushed

1/8 t pepper

Put chicken in crock pot. Mix remaining ingredients. Pour over chicken. Cover. Cook on "HIGH" heat 4-6 hours or until tender. Serve with cooked rice or noodles. Serves 6.

PORCUPINE MEATBALLS

2 beaten eggs
1/2 c uncooked white rice
1/4 c finely chopped onion
1 t salt
2 lb. ground beef
2 t Worcestershire sauce
2 10-3/4 oz. cans tomato soup

Combine egg, rice, onion, salt, beef and shape into meatballs. Place in 9" x 13" casserole dish. Mix Worcestershire sauce, soup, and 2/3 c water. Pour over meatballs. Bake, covered, in 325-degree oven for 1 hour. Serves 6.

Thursday

"BEST" MEATLOAF

1 egg
1 t salt
1/4 t pepper, basil, & thyme
2 T dry onion bits
1/4 c catsup
1-1/2 c soft bread crumbs
2 beef bouillon cubes
1 c boiling water
2 lb. ground beef

Beat egg lightly in bowl; add spices, catsup, & bread crumbs. Dissolve bouillon cubes in boiling water, add to bowl, and mix well. Break up beef, add to bowl, and mix lightly. Bake in loaf pan in 325-degree oven for 1 hour. Serve with scalloped potatoes. Serves 6.

PRIMARY FIVE-HOUR STEW

2 lb. beef stew meat, cut up
6 diced carrots
1/4 c dry onion bits
2 large diced potatoes
2 10-3/4 oz. cans tomato
   soup
2 cans water
2 t vinegar
2 t salt

Bake in 300-degree oven or crock pot on "HIGH" for five hours. Serves 6.

NO-PEEK CASSEROLE

1-1/2 lb. stew meat or
  2 lb. roast
1 10-3/4 oz. can cream of
  mushroom soup
2 T dry onion bits
2 bouillon cubes

Brown meat and add to rest of ingredients that have been mixed well. Cover tightly. Bake in 8" x 8" casserole dish for 3-1/2 hours (stew meat) or 5 hours (roast) in 300-degree oven. DON'T PEEK. Serve over mashed potatoes or cooked rice. Serves 6.

SPAGHETTI

ghetti, cooked
ained

sauce (pg. 40)

garine, sliced into

ingredients in
13" casserole
nd heat in
en for 25-30
ves 6.

MACARONI BEEF

2-1/2 c macaroni, cooked and drained

3 c *Italian sauce* (pg. 40)

1/2 c margarine, cubed

Mix above ingredients in 9" x 13" casserole dish, cover, and heat in 325-degree oven for 25-30 minutes. Serves 6.

LAZY DAY LASAGNA

In large bowl heat   3 c *Italian sauce (pg. 40)* and 3 c water

In small bowl mix 2 beaten eggs, 2 c cottage cheese, and 1 T parsley flakes

Shred 2 c mozzarella cheese onto plate

In 9" x 13" greased casserole dish layer sauce mixtures, 12 lasagna noodles, and cheese mixture. Top with shredded cheese. Bake in 325-degree oven for 1 hour tightly covered with foil. Remove from oven, uncover, and let sit 15 minutes. Serves 6.

Friday

MOCK STROGANOFF

4 c noodles, cooked and
  drained
3 c *Italian sauce* (pg. 40)
1/2 c mayonnaise

Mix sauce and mayonnaise together. Add noodles and mix again. Put above ingredients in 9" x 13" casserole dish and heat in 325-degree oven for 25-30 minutes. Serves 6.

SLOPPY JOES

3 c *taco meat* *(pg. 43)*, heated

Serve on hamburger buns. Garnish with dill pickles. Serves 6.

OVEN FRIED POTATOES

(to serve with hamburgers)

Slice 4 unpeeled, russet
potatoes into thin strips
lengthwise.

Mix in ziploc bag:
1 t salt
1 t onion powder
1 T salad oil
1 T melted margarine

Add potatoes to bag, seal bag, and
smother potatoes with spices and
oils. Place on cookie rack in large
cookie sheet. Sprinkle with paprika.
Bake 40 minutes in 400-degree
oven. Serve immediately. Serves 6.

MEATBALL HEROES

1 8-oz. can tomato sauce
1 T dry onion bits
1 beef bouillon cube
1 t sugar
1 lb. cooked ground beef

Simmer in saucepan for ten minutes. Serve on hot dog buns. Serves 6.

CHICKEN GUMBO BUGERS

1 lb. ground beef
2 T dry onion bits
3 T catsup
1 t prepared mustard
1 10-3/4 oz. can condensed
  chicken gumbo soup

Brown beef and onion. Stir in catsup, mustard and soup. Simmer until thickened. Spoon over hot dog buns. Serves 6.

FRENCH TOAST

8 eggs, beaten well
2 c milk
1 t salt
16-24 slices of slightly stale
    bread

Mix eggs, milk and salt. Heat grill to 300 degrees. Dip bread in egg mixture and fry on grill until lightly brown. Flip, top with granulated sugar, and fry until lightly brown. Serve with maple syrup. Serves 6.

HOOTENANY

Melt 1/4 c margarine in a
9" x 13" glass casserole
dish in 375-degree oven.

Combine in blender:
3/4 c water
1 c flour
1/3 c powdered milk
6-8 eggs

Pour mixture over melted butter
in glass dish. Bake in 375-
degree oven 15-20 minutes or
until lightly brown and puffy.
Serve with syrup. Serves 6.

Sunday

PANCAKES

3 c *Make-a-Mix* (pg. 42)
1/3 c sugar
3 eggs, beaten
1-1/2 c milk

Mix slightly and cook pancakes on greased grill heated to 300 degrees. Top with maple syrup. Serves 6.

Sunday

WAFFLES

3 c *Make-a-Mix* (pg. 42)
1/3 c sugar
3 eggs, beaten
1-1/2 c milk

Mix slightly and cook waffles in greased, heated waffle iron for 2-3 minutes. Top with maple syrup. Serves 6.

COFFEE CAKE

6 c *Make-a-Mix (pg. 42)*
2/3 c sugar
2 eggs, slightly beaten
2 c milk
2 t vanilla extract
1 c crumble topping
    (¼ c flour, ¼ c white sugar,
    ½ c brown sugar, 2 T
    melted margarine)

Mix dry ingredients. Combine wet ingredients. Fold together until blended. Put in three 9" greased pie pans and spread with topping. Bake in 350-degree oven for 20-25 minutes.

FRENCH BREAKFAST PUFFS

Mix:
  1-1/4 c sugar
  3-2/3 c flour
  3-3/4 t baking powder
  1-1/4 t salt
  Scant 3/4 t nutmeg

Beat together:
  3/4 c vegetable oil
  1-1/4 c milk
  3 eggs

Mix together wet and dry ingredients. Put in 24 muffin cups. Bake in 325-degree oven for 17-20 minutes. Serve warm.

ORANGE JULIUS MUFFINS

4 c flour

1-1/3 c white sugar

2 T baking powder

1-1/2 t salt

2/3 c vegetable oil

1-1/4 c orange juice

1-1/2 t vanilla

2 eggs

Combine dry ingredients in one bowl. Combine wet ingredients in another. Add wet to dry; stir to moisten. Put in 24 muffin cups. Bake in 325-degree oven 17-20 minutes. Serve warm.

BANNACK

3 c flour
2 t baking powder
3/4 t salt
3 T sugar
1-1/2 c water

Mix dry ingredients. Add water and mix until moist. Pour in two "pancakes" onto greased grill heated to 325 degrees. Spread outward with wooden spoons until flattened. Fry until lightly brown. Flip and fry again. Serve warm with margarine and jam. Serves 6.

GRANOLA

1-1/2 c white sugar
1-1/3 c margarine
2/3 c peanut butter
1/2 t salt
2 t vanilla
1 c water

Mix and heat above in 4-cup glass measuring cup 4 minutes on "HIGH".

Mix quickly with: 12 c rolled oats
                    1 t cinnamon

Spread onto two small, greased cookie sheets. Bake at 325 degrees for 25 minutes. Exchange cookie sheets on oven racks. Bake 10 minutes. Turn oven off and let granola dry for several hours. Break apart and store in airtight container. Make 24 cups.

ORANGE JULIUS

1-6 oz. can orange juice
    concentrate
2 c water
1/4 c sugar
2/3 c powdered milk
1 t vanilla extract
12-14 ice cubes

Mix in blender and serve.
Serves 4.

SWEDISH BREAD

6 c bread flour
1-1/2 T yeast
3/4 c sugar
1/2 t salt
2/3 c powdered milk
1-3/4 c hot water
3/4 c vegetable oil
15 cardamom seeds, crushed

Mix dry ingredients; add wet ingredients and crushed seeds. Mix in Kitchen Aid mixer for 5-7 minutes. Let rise until double and punch down two times. Shape into two oblong loaves and put on large, greased cookie sheet. Let rise until doubled. Preheat oven to 325-degrees. Bake bread 20-25 minutes or until light brown.

ITALIAN SAUCE

5 lb. ground beef, cooked
2 t *Italian seasoning mix*
 (pg. 41)
3 1" pieces frozen green
 pepper*
3 10-3/4 oz. cans tomato
 soup
6 8-oz. cans tomato sauce

Brown meat. Add other ingredients. Simmer over low heat for one hour. Store in containers in freezer.

Cut one green pepper into 1" pieces and store in freezer for convenient cooking of **Italian Sauce and **Taco Meat**.*

ITALIAN SEASONING MIX

1/8 t	1 t	dill weed
1/4 t	2 t	basil
1/2 t	1 T	fennel
1/4 t	2 t	garlic powder
1 t	3 T	onion powder
1/2 t	1 T	oregano
1/2 t	1 T	parsley flakes
1/8 t	1 t	pepper
1/4 t	2 t	salt

Mix all ingredients using electric blender.

Makes approximately:

4 t	9 T	mix

3 T equals strength of 1-1/4 oz. package *Italian seasoning mix.*

MAKE-A-MIX

26-1/2 c flour
3/4 c baking powder
3 T salt
2 T cream of tartar
1 T baking soda
4-2/3 c powdered milk
7 c shortening (1-3 lb. can)

Mix dry ingredients in very large bowl. Add one half of the shortening; mix well with electric mixer. Add rest of shortening, mix well. Store six months in sealed container in cool place.

TACO MEAT

5 lb. ground beef, cooked

3 t *taco seasoning mix* (pg. 44)

3 t sugar

3 t white vinegar

1-1/2 t Worcestershire sauce

3-1" pieces frozen green pepper

3-8 oz. cans tomato sauce

Brown meat. Add spices, peppers, sauce. Simmer over low heat for one hour. Store in containers and freeze until needed.

TACO SEASONING MIX

2 t	2 T	6 T	onion powder
1 t	1 T	3 T	garlic powder
1 t	1 T	3 T	paprika
1 t	1 T	3 T	oregano
1 t	1 T	3 T	sugar
½t	1½t	4½t	salt

Mix all ingredients using electric blender.

Makes approximately:
3 T   8 T   1 c   mix.

3 T equals strength of 1¼-oz. package *taco seasoning mix*.

Updating the Master Menu

As an endnote, about once a year, go through the "Master Menu" and make changes as necessary. Sometimes a popular meal loses face when someone leaves the home and the ones still at home are not as partial to it. Other times everyone becomes tired of a particular recipe and it should be relegated to the back of the recipe box.

Once the twenty-eight main meals are decided upon, a 3" x 5" recipe card might be prepared for each of these favorite meals. These are sorted and kept behind 3" x 5" card dividers labeled:

- Monday
- Tuesday
- Wednesday
- Thursday
- Friday
- Saturday
- Sunday

with four recipes behind each divider. Then this collection of recipes is put in the front of the recipe box. This simple procedure makes the recipes immediately accessible to the cook for the night. There will be no more looking for recipes in cookbooks, magazine clippings gathered in drawers, or index cards slipped somewhere into your recipe box.

This same method can be used for breakfast and lunch menus which will add even more convenience for all the cooks in the house.

Remember, once the "Master Menu" is in place and posted on the cupboard door, long-term purchases made to accommodate its use, and recipe cards made up for each of the meals, everything will be easier, more fun, and less stressful all around.

Try it, it will make more sense and bring greater organization to your kitchen than almost any other single change you can make. A "Master Menu" is for every home manager!

Master Menu Cookbook

Index

Index

Index

Master Menu Form – Main Menus

Day/Name	Main Dish	Bread	Vegetable	Fruit
Monday				
Quick				
Tuesday				
Mexican				
Wednesday				
Poultry				
Thursday				
Beef				
Friday				
Italian				
Saturday				
Easy				
Eggs				
Sunday				
Soup				
Breakfast				
for Dinner				
Worksheet #65				

Master Menu Form – Main Menus

Day/Name	Main Dish	Bread	Vegetable	Fruit
Monday				
Quick				
Tuesday				
Mexican				
Wednesday				
Poultry				
Thursday				
Beef				
Friday				
Italian				
Saturday				
Easy				
Eggs				
Sunday				
Soup				
Breakfast for Dinner				
Worksheet #65				

Master Menu Form – Main Menus

Day/Name	Main Dish	Bread	Vegetable	Fruit
Monday				
Quick				
Tuesday				
Mexican				
Wednesday				
Poultry				
Thursday				
Beef				
Friday				
Italian				
Saturday				
Easy				
Eggs				
Sunday				
Soup				
Breakfast				
for Dinner				
Worksheet #65				

Master Menu Form – Breakfasts and Lunches

Day	Breakfast	Day	Lunch
Monday		Monday	
Tuesday		Tuesday	
Wednesday		Wednesday	
Thursday		Thursday	
Friday		Friday	
Saturday		Saturday	
Sunday		Sunday	
Worksheet #67			

Master Menu Form – Breakfasts and Lunches

Day	Breakfast	Day	Lunch
Monday		Monday	
Tuesday		Tuesday	
Wednesday		Wednesday	
Thursday		Thursday	
Friday		Friday	
Saturday		Saturday	
Sunday		Sunday	
Worksheet #67			

Master Menu Form – Breakfasts and Lunches

Day	Breakfast	Day	Lunch
Monday		Monday	
Tuesday		Tuesday	
Wednesday		Wednesday	
Thursday		Thursday	
Friday		Friday	
Saturday		Saturday	
Sunday		Sunday	
Worksheet #67